MW01096866

the Complete FELINE HEALTH RECORD Book

Feline Health Record © 2021 Sosha Publishing

FELINE INFORMATION

NAME:

BIRTHDATE:	GENDER:
BREED:	SPAYED/NEUTERED:
COAT COLOR:	EYE COLOR:
MARKINGS:	DECLAWED:

OWNER(S):

ADDRESS:

PHONE:	CELL:

E-MAIL:

BREEDER/SHELTER:

DATE ACQUIRED:	REGISTERED NAME:
SIRE:	DAM:
TICA REGISTRY #	REGISTRATION TYPE:
CFA REGISTRY #	DNA #
MICROCHIP #	COMPANY:

VETERINARIAN:

EMERGENCY VET:

FELINE INFORMATION

WEIGHT	DATE	MEDICAL HISTORY
8 WEEKS:		
12 WEEKS:		
16 WEEKS:		
20 WEEKS:		
6 MONTHS:		
1 YEAR:		
2 YEARS:		
3 YEARS:		
4 YEARS:		
5 YEARS:		
6 YEARS:		
7 YEARS:		
8 YEARS:		
9 YEARS:		
10 YEARS:		
11 YEARS:		
12 YEARS:		
13 YEARS:		
14 YEARS:		

FELINE INFORMATION

WEIGHT		DATE	MEDICAL HISTORY
15 YEARS:			
16 YEARS:			
17 YEARS:			
18 YEARS:			
19 YEARS:			
20 YEARS:			

NOTES

VACCINATIONS

VACCINE	DATES					NOTE
FVRCP						
RABIES						
FeLV						
BORDETELLA						
FIV						
CHLAMYDIA FELIS						
FIP						

OTHER TREATMENTS

DEWORMING						
FLEA & TICK						

VACCINATIONS

VACCINE	DATES					NOTE
FVRCP						
RABIES						
FeLV						
BORDETELLA						
FIV						
CHLAMYDIA FELIS						
FIP						

OTHER TREATMENTS

DEWORMING						
FLEA & TICK						

VACCINATIONS

VACCINE	DATES					NOTE
FVRCP						
RABIES						
FeLV						
BORDETELLA						
FIV						
CHLAMYDIA FELIS						
FIP						

OTHER TREATMENTS

DEWORMING						
FLEA & TICK						

VACCINATIONS

VACCINE	DATES					NOTE
FVRCP						
RABIES						
FeLV						
BORDETELLA						
FIV						
CHLAMYDIA FELIS						
FIP						

OTHER TREATMENTS

DEWORMING						
FLEA & TICK						

VACCINATIONS

VACCINE	DATES					NOTE
FVRCP						
RABIES						
FeLV						
BORDETELLA						
FIV						
CHLAMYDIA FELIS						
FIP						

OTHER TREATMENTS

DEWORMING						
FLEA & TICK						

VET VISITATION LOG

DATE:	TIME:	VETERINARIAN:

REASON FOR VISIT:

_____

_____

_____

_____

TREATMENT PLAN:

_____

_____

_____

_____

MEDICATIONS:

_____

VACCINATIONS:

_____

VISIT NOTES

_____

_____

_____

_____

_____

_____

VET VISITATION LOG

DATE:	TIME:	VETERINARIAN:

REASON FOR VISIT:

TREATMENT PLAN:

MEDICATIONS:

VACCINATIONS:

VISIT NOTES

VET VISITATION LOG

DATE:	TIME:	VETERINARIAN:

REASON FOR VISIT:

TREATMENT PLAN:

MEDICATIONS:

VACCINATIONS:

VISIT NOTES

VET VISITATION LOG

DATE:	TIME:	VETERINARIAN:

REASON FOR VISIT:

TREATMENT PLAN:

MEDICATIONS:

VACCINATIONS:

VISIT NOTES

VET VISITATION LOG

DATE:	TIME:	VETERINARIAN:

REASON FOR VISIT:

_____

_____

_____

_____

TREATMENT PLAN:

_____

_____

_____

_____

MEDICATIONS:

VACCINATIONS:

_____

VISIT NOTES

_____

_____

_____

_____

_____

_____

VET VISITATION LOG

DATE:	TIME:	VETERINARIAN:

REASON FOR VISIT:

TREATMENT PLAN:

MEDICATIONS:

VACCINATIONS:

VISIT NOTES

VET VISITATION LOG

DATE:	TIME:	VETERINARIAN:

REASON FOR VISIT:

_____

_____

_____

_____

TREATMENT PLAN:

_____

_____

_____

_____

MEDICATIONS:

VACCINATIONS:

_____

VISIT NOTES

_____

_____

_____

_____

_____

VET VISITATION LOG

DATE:	TIME:	VETERINARIAN:

REASON FOR VISIT:

TREATMENT PLAN:

MEDICATIONS:

VACCINATIONS:

VISIT NOTES

VET VISITATION LOG

DATE:	TIME:	VETERINARIAN:

REASON FOR VISIT:

_____

_____

_____

_____

TREATMENT PLAN:

_____

_____

_____

_____

MEDICATIONS:

VACCINATIONS:

_____

VISIT NOTES

_____

_____

_____

_____

_____

_____

VET VISITATION LOG

DATE:	TIME:	VETERINARIAN:

REASON FOR VISIT:

_____

_____

_____

_____

TREATMENT PLAN:

_____

_____

_____

_____

MEDICATIONS:

VACCINATIONS:

_____

VISIT NOTES

_____

_____

_____

_____

_____

_____

VET VISITATION LOG

DATE:	TIME:	VETERINARIAN:

REASON FOR VISIT:

_____

_____

_____

_____

TREATMENT PLAN:

_____

_____

_____

_____

MEDICATIONS:

VACCINATIONS:

_____

VISIT NOTES

_____

_____

_____

_____

_____

VET VISITATION LOG

DATE:	TIME:	VETERINARIAN:

REASON FOR VISIT:

TREATMENT PLAN:

MEDICATIONS:

VACCINATIONS:

VISIT NOTES

VET VISITATION LOG

DATE:	TIME:	VETERINARIAN:

REASON FOR VISIT:

TREATMENT PLAN:

MEDICATIONS:

VACCINATIONS:

VISIT NOTES

VET VISITATION LOG

DATE:	TIME:	VETERINARIAN:

REASON FOR VISIT:

TREATMENT PLAN:

MEDICATIONS:

VACCINATIONS:

VISIT NOTES

VET VISITATION LOG

DATE:	TIME:	VETERINARIAN:

REASON FOR VISIT:

TREATMENT PLAN:

MEDICATIONS:

VACCINATIONS:

VISIT NOTES

VET VISITATION LOG

DATE:	TIME:	VETERINARIAN:

REASON FOR VISIT:

TREATMENT PLAN:

MEDICATIONS:

VACCINATIONS:

VISIT NOTES

VET VISITATION LOG

DATE:	TIME:	VETERINARIAN:

REASON FOR VISIT:

TREATMENT PLAN:

MEDICATIONS:

VACCINATIONS:

VISIT NOTES

VET VISITATION LOG

DATE:	TIME:	VETERINARIAN:

REASON FOR VISIT:

TREATMENT PLAN:

MEDICATIONS:

VACCINATIONS:

VISIT NOTES

VET VISITATION LOG

DATE:	TIME:	VETERINARIAN:

REASON FOR VISIT:

_____

_____

_____

_____

_____

TREATMENT PLAN:

_____

_____

_____

_____

MEDICATIONS:

_____

VACCINATIONS:

_____

VISIT NOTES

_____

_____

_____

_____

_____

VET VISITATION LOG

DATE:	TIME:	VETERINARIAN:

REASON FOR VISIT:

TREATMENT PLAN:

MEDICATIONS:

VACCINATIONS:

VISIT NOTES

VET VISITATION LOG

DATE:	TIME:	VETERINARIAN:

REASON FOR VISIT:

TREATMENT PLAN:

MEDICATIONS:

VACCINATIONS:

VISIT NOTES

VET VISITATION LOG

DATE:	TIME:	VETERINARIAN:

REASON FOR VISIT:

TREATMENT PLAN:

MEDICATIONS:

VACCINATIONS:

VISIT NOTES

VET VISITATION LOG

DATE:	TIME:	VETERINARIAN:

REASON FOR VISIT:

_____

_____

_____

_____

TREATMENT PLAN:

_____

_____

_____

_____

MEDICATIONS:

VACCINATIONS:

_____

VISIT NOTES

_____

_____

_____

_____

_____

VET VISITATION LOG

DATE:	TIME:	VETERINARIAN:

REASON FOR VISIT:

TREATMENT PLAN:

MEDICATIONS:

VACCINATIONS:

VISIT NOTES

VET VISITATION LOG

DATE:	TIME:	VETERINARIAN:

REASON FOR VISIT:

_____

_____

_____

_____

TREATMENT PLAN:

_____

_____

_____

_____

MEDICATIONS:

_____

VACCINATIONS:

_____

VISIT NOTES

_____

_____

_____

_____

_____

VET VISITATION LOG

DATE:	TIME:	VETERINARIAN:

REASON FOR VISIT:

_____

_____

_____

_____

TREATMENT PLAN:

_____

_____

_____

_____

MEDICATIONS:

VACCINATIONS:

_____

VISIT NOTES

_____

_____

_____

_____

_____

VET VISITATION LOG

DATE:	TIME:	VETERINARIAN:

REASON FOR VISIT:

TREATMENT PLAN:

MEDICATIONS:

VACCINATIONS:

VISIT NOTES

VET VISITATION LOG

DATE:	TIME:	VETERINARIAN:

REASON FOR VISIT:

TREATMENT PLAN:

MEDICATIONS:

VACCINATIONS:

VISIT NOTES

VET VISITATION LOG

DATE:	TIME:	VETERINARIAN:

REASON FOR VISIT:

_____

_____

_____

_____

TREATMENT PLAN:

_____

_____

_____

_____

MEDICATIONS:

VACCINATIONS:

VISIT NOTES

_____

_____

_____

_____

_____

VET VISITATION LOG

DATE:	TIME:	VETERINARIAN:

REASON FOR VISIT:

TREATMENT PLAN:

MEDICATIONS:

VACCINATIONS:

VISIT NOTES

VET VISITATION LOG

DATE:	TIME:	VETERINARIAN:

REASON FOR VISIT:

TREATMENT PLAN:

MEDICATIONS:

VACCINATIONS:

VISIT NOTES

VET VISITATION LOG

DATE:	TIME:	VETERINARIAN:

REASON FOR VISIT:

TREATMENT PLAN:

MEDICATIONS:

VACCINATIONS:

VISIT NOTES

VET VISITATION LOG

DATE:	TIME:	VETERINARIAN:

REASON FOR VISIT:

_____

_____

_____

_____

_____

TREATMENT PLAN:

_____

_____

_____

_____

_____

MEDICATIONS:

_____

VACCINATIONS:

_____

_____

VISIT NOTES

_____

_____

_____

_____

_____

_____

VET VISITATION LOG

DATE:	TIME:	VETERINARIAN:

REASON FOR VISIT:

TREATMENT PLAN:

MEDICATIONS:

VACCINATIONS:

VISIT NOTES

VET VISITATION LOG

DATE:	TIME:	VETERINARIAN:

REASON FOR VISIT:

TREATMENT PLAN:

MEDICATIONS:

VACCINATIONS:

VISIT NOTES

VET VISITATION LOG

DATE:	TIME:	VETERINARIAN:

REASON FOR VISIT:

TREATMENT PLAN:

MEDICATIONS:

VACCINATIONS:

VISIT NOTES

VET VISITATION LOG

DATE:	TIME:	VETERINARIAN:

REASON FOR VISIT:

TREATMENT PLAN:

MEDICATIONS:

VACCINATIONS:

VISIT NOTES

VET VISITATION LOG

DATE:	TIME:	VETERINARIAN:

REASON FOR VISIT:

TREATMENT PLAN:

MEDICATIONS:

VACCINATIONS:

VISIT NOTES

VET VISITATION LOG

DATE:	TIME:	VETERINARIAN:

REASON FOR VISIT:

TREATMENT PLAN:

MEDICATIONS:

VACCINATIONS:

VISIT NOTES

VET VISITATION LOG

DATE:	TIME:	VETERINARIAN:

REASON FOR VISIT:

TREATMENT PLAN:

MEDICATIONS:

VACCINATIONS:

VISIT NOTES

FELINE

#2

FELINE

#2

FELINE INFORMATION

NAME:

BIRTHDATE:	GENDER:
BREED:	SPAYED/NEUTERED:
COAT COLOR:	EYE COLOR:
MARKINGS:	DECLAWED:

OWNER(S):

ADDRESS:

PHONE:	CELL:

E-MAIL:

BREEDER/SHELTER:

DATE ACQUIRED:	REGISTERED NAME:
SIRE:	DAM:
TICA REGISTRY #	REGISTRATION TYPE:
CFA REGISTRY #	DNA #
MICROCHIP #	COMPANY:

VETERINARIAN:

EMERGENCY VET:

FELINE INFORMATION

WEIGHT	DATE	MEDICAL HISTORY
8 WEEKS:		
12 WEEKS:		
16 WEEKS:		
20 WEEKS:		
6 MONTHS:		
1 YEAR:		
2 YEARS:		
3 YEARS:		
4 YEARS:		
5 YEARS:		
6 YEARS:		
7 YEARS:		
8 YEARS:		
9 YEARS:		
10 YEARS:		
11 YEARS:		
12 YEARS:		
13 YEARS:		
14 YEARS:		

FELINE INFORMATION

WEIGHT		DATE	MEDICAL HISTORY
15 YEARS:			
16 YEARS:			
17 YEARS:			
18 YEARS:			
19 YEARS:			
20 YEARS:			

NOTES

VACCINATIONS

VACCINE	DATES					NOTE
FVRCP						
RABIES						
FeLV						
BORDETELLA						
FIV						
CHLAMYDIA FELIS						
FIP						
OTHER TREATMENTS						
DEWORMING						
FLEA & TICK						

VACCINATIONS

VACCINE	DATES					NOTE
FVRCP						
RABIES						
FeLV						
BORDETELLA						
FIV						
CHLAMYDIA FELIS						
FIP						

OTHER TREATMENTS

DEWORMING						
FLEA & TICK						

VACCINATIONS

VACCINE	DATES					NOTE
FVRCP						
RABIES						
FeLV						
BORDETELLA						
FIV						
CHLAMYDIA FELIS						
FIP						
OTHER TREATMENTS						
DEWORMING						
FLEA & TICK						

VACCINATIONS

VACCINE	DATES					NOTE
FVRCP						
RABIES						
FeLV						
BORDETELLA						
FIV						
CHLAMYDIA FELIS						
FIP						

OTHER TREATMENTS

DEWORMING						
FLEA & TICK						

VACCINATIONS

VACCINE	DATES					NOTE
FVRCP						
RABIES						
FeLV						
BORDETELLA						
FIV						
CHLAMYDIA FELIS						
FIP						

OTHER TREATMENTS

DEWORMING					
FLEA & TICK					

VET VISITATION LOG

DATE:	TIME:	VETERINARIAN:

REASON FOR VISIT:

_____

_____

_____

_____

TREATMENT PLAN:

_____

_____

_____

_____

MEDICATIONS:

VACCINATIONS:

_____

VISIT NOTES

_____

_____

_____

_____

_____

_____

VET VISITATION LOG

DATE:	TIME:	VETERINARIAN:

REASON FOR VISIT:

TREATMENT PLAN:

MEDICATIONS:

VACCINATIONS:

VISIT NOTES

VET VISITATION LOG

DATE:	TIME:	VETERINARIAN:

REASON FOR VISIT:

TREATMENT PLAN:

MEDICATIONS:

VACCINATIONS:

VISIT NOTES

VET VISITATION LOG

DATE:	TIME:	VETERINARIAN:

REASON FOR VISIT:

TREATMENT PLAN:

MEDICATIONS:

VACCINATIONS:

VISIT NOTES

VET VISITATION LOG

DATE:	TIME:	VETERINARIAN:

REASON FOR VISIT:

_____

_____

_____

_____

_____

TREATMENT PLAN:

_____

_____

_____

_____

MEDICATIONS:

VACCINATIONS:

_____

VISIT NOTES

_____

_____

_____

_____

_____

_____

VET VISITATION LOG

DATE:	TIME:	VETERINARIAN:

REASON FOR VISIT:

TREATMENT PLAN:

MEDICATIONS:

VACCINATIONS:

VISIT NOTES

VET VISITATION LOG

DATE:	TIME:	VETERINARIAN:

REASON FOR VISIT:

TREATMENT PLAN:

MEDICATIONS:

VACCINATIONS:

VISIT NOTES

VET VISITATION LOG

DATE:	TIME:	VETERINARIAN:

REASON FOR VISIT:

TREATMENT PLAN:

MEDICATIONS:

VACCINATIONS:

VISIT NOTES

VET VISITATION LOG

DATE:	TIME:	VETERINARIAN:

REASON FOR VISIT:

TREATMENT PLAN:

MEDICATIONS:

VACCINATIONS:

VISIT NOTES

VET VISITATION LOG

DATE:	TIME:	VETERINARIAN:

REASON FOR VISIT:

TREATMENT PLAN:

MEDICATIONS:

VACCINATIONS:

VISIT NOTES

VET VISITATION LOG

DATE:	TIME:	VETERINARIAN:

REASON FOR VISIT:

_____

_____

_____

_____

TREATMENT PLAN:

_____

_____

_____

_____

MEDICATIONS:

_____

VACCINATIONS:

_____

VISIT NOTES

_____

_____

_____

_____

_____

_____

VET VISITATION LOG

DATE:	TIME:	VETERINARIAN:

REASON FOR VISIT:

TREATMENT PLAN:

MEDICATIONS:

VACCINATIONS:

VISIT NOTES

VET VISITATION LOG

DATE:	TIME:	VETERINARIAN:

REASON FOR VISIT:

TREATMENT PLAN:

MEDICATIONS:

VACCINATIONS:

VISIT NOTES

VET VISITATION LOG

DATE:	TIME:	VETERINARIAN:

REASON FOR VISIT:

TREATMENT PLAN:

MEDICATIONS:

VACCINATIONS:

VISIT NOTES

VET VISITATION LOG

DATE:	TIME:	VETERINARIAN:

REASON FOR VISIT:

TREATMENT PLAN:

MEDICATIONS:

VACCINATIONS:

VISIT NOTES

VET VISITATION LOG

DATE:	TIME:	VETERINARIAN:

REASON FOR VISIT:

_____

_____

_____

_____

TREATMENT PLAN:

_____

_____

_____

_____

MEDICATIONS:

VACCINATIONS:

_____

VISIT NOTES

_____

_____

_____

_____

_____

_____

VET VISITATION LOG

DATE:	TIME:	VETERINARIAN:

REASON FOR VISIT:

TREATMENT PLAN:

MEDICATIONS:

VACCINATIONS:

VISIT NOTES

VET VISITATION LOG

DATE:	TIME:	VETERINARIAN:

REASON FOR VISIT:

TREATMENT PLAN:

MEDICATIONS:

VACCINATIONS:

VISIT NOTES

VET VISITATION LOG

DATE:	TIME:	VETERINARIAN:

REASON FOR VISIT:

TREATMENT PLAN:

MEDICATIONS:

VACCINATIONS:

VISIT NOTES

VET VISITATION LOG

DATE:	TIME:	VETERINARIAN:

REASON FOR VISIT:

TREATMENT PLAN:

MEDICATIONS:

VACCINATIONS:

VISIT NOTES

VET VISITATION LOG

DATE:	TIME:	VETERINARIAN:

REASON FOR VISIT:

TREATMENT PLAN:

MEDICATIONS:

VACCINATIONS:

VISIT NOTES

VET VISITATION LOG

DATE:	TIME:	VETERINARIAN:

REASON FOR VISIT:

TREATMENT PLAN:

MEDICATIONS:

VACCINATIONS:

VISIT NOTES

VET VISITATION LOG

DATE:	TIME:	VETERINARIAN:

REASON FOR VISIT:

TREATMENT PLAN:

MEDICATIONS:

VACCINATIONS:

VISIT NOTES

VET VISITATION LOG

DATE:	TIME:	VETERINARIAN:

REASON FOR VISIT:

TREATMENT PLAN:

MEDICATIONS:

VACCINATIONS:

VISIT NOTES

VET VISITATION LOG

DATE:	TIME:	VETERINARIAN:

REASON FOR VISIT:

TREATMENT PLAN:

MEDICATIONS:

VACCINATIONS:

VISIT NOTES

VET VISITATION LOG

DATE:	TIME:	VETERINARIAN:

REASON FOR VISIT:

_____

_____

_____

_____

TREATMENT PLAN:

_____

_____

_____

_____

MEDICATIONS:

VACCINATIONS:

VISIT NOTES

_____

_____

_____

_____

_____

_____

VET VISITATION LOG

DATE:	TIME:	VETERINARIAN:

REASON FOR VISIT:

_____

_____

_____

_____

TREATMENT PLAN:

_____

_____

_____

_____

MEDICATIONS:

VACCINATIONS:

VISIT NOTES

_____

_____

_____

_____

_____

VET VISITATION LOG

DATE:	TIME:	VETERINARIAN:

REASON FOR VISIT:

_____

_____

_____

_____

TREATMENT PLAN:

_____

_____

_____

_____

MEDICATIONS:

_____

VACCINATIONS:

_____

VISIT NOTES

_____

_____

_____

_____

_____

_____

VET VISITATION LOG

DATE:	TIME:	VETERINARIAN:

REASON FOR VISIT:

TREATMENT PLAN:

MEDICATIONS:

VACCINATIONS:

VISIT NOTES

VET VISITATION LOG

DATE:	TIME:	VETERINARIAN:

REASON FOR VISIT:

TREATMENT PLAN:

MEDICATIONS:

VACCINATIONS:

VISIT NOTES

VET VISITATION LOG

DATE:	TIME:	VETERINARIAN:

REASON FOR VISIT:

TREATMENT PLAN:

MEDICATIONS:

VACCINATIONS:

VISIT NOTES

VET VISITATION LOG

DATE:	TIME:	VETERINARIAN:

REASON FOR VISIT:

_____

_____

_____

_____

TREATMENT PLAN:

_____

_____

_____

_____

MEDICATIONS:

VACCINATIONS:

VISIT NOTES

_____

_____

_____

_____

_____

_____

VET VISITATION LOG

DATE:	TIME:	VETERINARIAN:

REASON FOR VISIT:

TREATMENT PLAN:

MEDICATIONS:

VACCINATIONS:

VISIT NOTES

VET VISITATION LOG

DATE:	TIME:	VETERINARIAN:

REASON FOR VISIT:

TREATMENT PLAN:

MEDICATIONS:

VACCINATIONS:

VISIT NOTES

VET VISITATION LOG

DATE:	TIME:	VETERINARIAN:

REASON FOR VISIT:

_____

_____

_____

_____

TREATMENT PLAN:

_____

_____

_____

MEDICATIONS:

VACCINATIONS:

VISIT NOTES

_____

_____

_____

_____

_____

_____

VET VISITATION LOG

DATE:	TIME:	VETERINARIAN:

REASON FOR VISIT:

TREATMENT PLAN:

MEDICATIONS:

VACCINATIONS:

VISIT NOTES

VET VISITATION LOG

DATE:	TIME:	VETERINARIAN:

REASON FOR VISIT:

TREATMENT PLAN:

MEDICATIONS:

VACCINATIONS:

VISIT NOTES

VET VISITATION LOG

DATE:	TIME:	VETERINARIAN:

REASON FOR VISIT:

TREATMENT PLAN:

MEDICATIONS:

VACCINATIONS:

VISIT NOTES

VET VISITATION LOG

DATE:	TIME:	VETERINARIAN:

REASON FOR VISIT:

TREATMENT PLAN:

MEDICATIONS:

VACCINATIONS:

VISIT NOTES

VET VISITATION LOG

DATE:	TIME:	VETERINARIAN:

REASON FOR VISIT:

_____

_____

_____

_____

TREATMENT PLAN:

_____

_____

_____

_____

MEDICATIONS:

_____

VACCINATIONS:

_____

VISIT NOTES

_____

_____

_____

_____

_____

_____

FELINE

3

FELINE

3

FELINE INFORMATION

NAME:

BIRTHDATE:	GENDER:
BREED:	SPAYED/NEUTERED:
COAT COLOR:	EYE COLOR:
MARKINGS:	DECLAWED:

OWNER(S):

ADDRESS:

PHONE:	CELL:

E-MAIL:

BREEDER/SHELTER:

DATE ACQUIRED:	REGISTERED NAME:
SIRE:	DAM:
TICA REGISTRY #	REGISTRATION TYPE:
CFA REGISTRY #	DNA #
MICROCHIP #	COMPANY:

VETERINARIAN:

EMERGENCY VET:

FELINE INFORMATION

WEIGHT	DATE	MEDICAL HISTORY
8 WEEKS:		
12 WEEKS:		
16 WEEKS:		
20 WEEKS:		
6 MONTHS:		
1 YEAR:		
2 YEARS:		
3 YEARS:		
4 YEARS:		
5 YEARS:		
6 YEARS:		
7 YEARS:		
8 YEARS:		
9 YEARS:		
10 YEARS:		
11 YEARS:		
12 YEARS:		
13 YEARS:		
14 YEARS:		

FELINE INFORMATION

WEIGHT
15 YEARS:
16 YEARS:
17 YEARS:
18 YEARS:
19 YEARS:
20 YEARS:

NOTES

DATE	MEDICAL HISTORY

VACCINATIONS

VACCINE	DATES					NOTE
FVRCP						
RABIES						
FeLV						
BORDETELLA						
FIV						
CHLAMYDIA FELIS						
FIP						

OTHER TREATMENTS

DEWORMING						
FLEA & TICK						

VACCINATIONS

VACCINE	DATES					NOTE
FVRCP						
RABIES						
FeLV						
BORDETELLA						
FIV						
CHLAMYDIA FELIS						
FIP						

OTHER TREATMENTS

DEWORMING						
FLEA & TICK						

VACCINATIONS

VACCINE	DATES					NOTE
FVRCP						
RABIES						
FeLV						
BORDETELLA						
FIV						
CHLAMYDIA FELIS						
FIP						

OTHER TREATMENTS

DEWORMING						
FLEA & TICK						

VACCINATIONS

VACCINE	DATES					NOTE
FVRCP						
RABIES						
FeLV						
BORDETELLA						
FIV						
CHLAMYDIA FELIS						
FIP						
OTHER TREATMENTS						
DEWORMING						
FLEA & TICK						

VACCINATIONS

VACCINE	DATES					NOTE
FVRCP						
RABIES						
FeLV						
BORDETELLA						
FIV						
CHLAMYDIA FELIS						
FIP						

OTHER TREATMENTS

DEWORMING						
FLEA & TICK						

VET VISITATION LOG

DATE:	TIME:	VETERINARIAN:

REASON FOR VISIT:

TREATMENT PLAN:

MEDICATIONS:

VACCINATIONS:

VISIT NOTES

VET VISITATION LOG

DATE:	TIME:	VETERINARIAN:

REASON FOR VISIT:

TREATMENT PLAN:

MEDICATIONS:

VACCINATIONS:

VISIT NOTES

VET VISITATION LOG

DATE:	TIME:	VETERINARIAN:

REASON FOR VISIT:

TREATMENT PLAN:

MEDICATIONS:

VACCINATIONS:

VISIT NOTES

VET VISITATION LOG

DATE:	TIME:	VETERINARIAN:

REASON FOR VISIT:

TREATMENT PLAN:

MEDICATIONS:

VACCINATIONS:

VISIT NOTES

VET VISITATION LOG

DATE:	TIME:	VETERINARIAN:

REASON FOR VISIT:

TREATMENT PLAN:

MEDICATIONS:

VACCINATIONS:

VISIT NOTES

VET VISITATION LOG

DATE:	TIME:	VETERINARIAN:

REASON FOR VISIT:

_____

_____

_____

_____

TREATMENT PLAN:

_____

_____

_____

_____

MEDICATIONS:

VACCINATIONS:

VISIT NOTES

_____

_____

_____

_____

_____

_____

VET VISITATION LOG

DATE:	TIME:	VETERINARIAN:

REASON FOR VISIT:

TREATMENT PLAN:

MEDICATIONS:

VACCINATIONS:

VISIT NOTES

VET VISITATION LOG

DATE:	TIME:	VETERINARIAN:

REASON FOR VISIT:

TREATMENT PLAN:

MEDICATIONS:

VACCINATIONS:

VISIT NOTES

VET VISITATION LOG

DATE:	TIME:	VETERINARIAN:

REASON FOR VISIT:

TREATMENT PLAN:

MEDICATIONS:

VACCINATIONS:

VISIT NOTES

VET VISITATION LOG

DATE:	TIME:	VETERINARIAN:

REASON FOR VISIT:

TREATMENT PLAN:

MEDICATIONS:

VACCINATIONS:

VISIT NOTES

VET VISITATION LOG

DATE:	TIME:	VETERINARIAN:

REASON FOR VISIT:

TREATMENT PLAN:

MEDICATIONS:

VACCINATIONS:

VISIT NOTES

VET VISITATION LOG

DATE:	TIME:	VETERINARIAN:

REASON FOR VISIT:

TREATMENT PLAN:

MEDICATIONS:

VACCINATIONS:

VISIT NOTES

VET VISITATION LOG

DATE:	TIME:	VETERINARIAN:

REASON FOR VISIT:

TREATMENT PLAN:

MEDICATIONS:

VACCINATIONS:

VISIT NOTES

VET VISITATION LOG

DATE:	TIME:	VETERINARIAN:

REASON FOR VISIT:

_____

_____

_____

_____

TREATMENT PLAN:

_____

_____

_____

_____

MEDICATIONS:

_____

VACCINATIONS:

_____

VISIT NOTES

_____

_____

_____

_____

_____

_____

VET VISITATION LOG

DATE:	TIME:	VETERINARIAN:

REASON FOR VISIT:

TREATMENT PLAN:

MEDICATIONS:

VACCINATIONS:

VISIT NOTES

VET VISITATION LOG

DATE:	TIME:	VETERINARIAN:

REASON FOR VISIT:

TREATMENT PLAN:

MEDICATIONS:

VACCINATIONS:

VISIT NOTES

VET VISITATION LOG

DATE:	TIME:	VETERINARIAN:

REASON FOR VISIT:

TREATMENT PLAN:

MEDICATIONS:

VACCINATIONS:

VISIT NOTES

VET VISITATION LOG

DATE:	TIME:	VETERINARIAN:

REASON FOR VISIT:

TREATMENT PLAN:

MEDICATIONS:

VACCINATIONS:

VISIT NOTES

VET VISITATION LOG

DATE:	TIME:	VETERINARIAN:

REASON FOR VISIT:

_____

_____

_____

_____

TREATMENT PLAN:

_____

_____

_____

_____

MEDICATIONS:

VACCINATIONS:

VISIT NOTES

_____

_____

_____

_____

_____

VET VISITATION LOG

DATE:	TIME:	VETERINARIAN:

REASON FOR VISIT:

TREATMENT PLAN:

MEDICATIONS:

VACCINATIONS:

VISIT NOTES

VET VISITATION LOG

DATE:	TIME:	VETERINARIAN:

REASON FOR VISIT:

_____

_____

_____

_____

TREATMENT PLAN:

_____

_____

_____

_____

MEDICATIONS:

VACCINATIONS:

_____

VISIT NOTES

_____

_____

_____

_____

_____

_____

VET VISITATION LOG

DATE:	TIME:	VETERINARIAN:

REASON FOR VISIT:

TREATMENT PLAN:

MEDICATIONS:

VACCINATIONS:

VISIT NOTES

VET VISITATION LOG

DATE:	TIME:	VETERINARIAN:

REASON FOR VISIT:

TREATMENT PLAN:

MEDICATIONS:

VACCINATIONS:

VISIT NOTES

VET VISITATION LOG

DATE:	TIME:	VETERINARIAN:

REASON FOR VISIT:

TREATMENT PLAN:

MEDICATIONS:

VACCINATIONS:

VISIT NOTES

VET VISITATION LOG

DATE:	TIME:	VETERINARIAN:

REASON FOR VISIT:

TREATMENT PLAN:

MEDICATIONS:

VACCINATIONS:

VISIT NOTES

VET VISITATION LOG

DATE:	TIME:	VETERINARIAN:

REASON FOR VISIT:

TREATMENT PLAN:

MEDICATIONS:

VACCINATIONS:

VISIT NOTES

VET VISITATION LOG

DATE:	TIME:	VETERINARIAN:

REASON FOR VISIT:

TREATMENT PLAN:

MEDICATIONS:

VACCINATIONS:

VISIT NOTES

VET VISITATION LOG

DATE:	TIME:	VETERINARIAN:

REASON FOR VISIT:

TREATMENT PLAN:

MEDICATIONS:

VACCINATIONS:

VISIT NOTES

VET VISITATION LOG

DATE:	TIME:	VETERINARIAN:

REASON FOR VISIT:

TREATMENT PLAN:

MEDICATIONS:

VACCINATIONS:

VISIT NOTES

VET VISITATION LOG

DATE:	TIME:	VETERINARIAN:

REASON FOR VISIT:

TREATMENT PLAN:

MEDICATIONS:

VACCINATIONS:

VISIT NOTES

VET VISITATION LOG

DATE:	TIME:	VETERINARIAN:

REASON FOR VISIT:

TREATMENT PLAN:

MEDICATIONS:

VACCINATIONS:

VISIT NOTES

VET VISITATION LOG

DATE:	TIME:	VETERINARIAN:

REASON FOR VISIT:

TREATMENT PLAN:

MEDICATIONS:

VACCINATIONS:

VISIT NOTES

VET VISITATION LOG

DATE:	TIME:	VETERINARIAN:

REASON FOR VISIT:

TREATMENT PLAN:

MEDICATIONS:

VACCINATIONS:

VISIT NOTES

VET VISITATION LOG

DATE:	TIME:	VETERINARIAN:

REASON FOR VISIT:

TREATMENT PLAN:

MEDICATIONS:

VACCINATIONS:

VISIT NOTES

VET VISITATION LOG

DATE:	TIME:	VETERINARIAN:

REASON FOR VISIT:

TREATMENT PLAN:

MEDICATIONS:

VACCINATIONS:

VISIT NOTES

VET VISITATION LOG

DATE:	TIME:	VETERINARIAN:

REASON FOR VISIT:

TREATMENT PLAN:

MEDICATIONS:

VACCINATIONS:

VISIT NOTES

VET VISITATION LOG

DATE:	TIME:	VETERINARIAN:

REASON FOR VISIT:

TREATMENT PLAN:

MEDICATIONS:

VACCINATIONS:

VISIT NOTES

VET VISITATION LOG

DATE:	TIME:	VETERINARIAN:

REASON FOR VISIT:

_____

_____

_____

_____

TREATMENT PLAN:

_____

_____

_____

_____

MEDICATIONS:

_____

VACCINATIONS:

_____

VISIT NOTES

_____

_____

_____

_____

_____

_____

VET VISITATION LOG

DATE:	TIME:	VETERINARIAN:

REASON FOR VISIT:

TREATMENT PLAN:

MEDICATIONS:

VACCINATIONS:

VISIT NOTES

VET VISITATION LOG

DATE:	TIME:	VETERINARIAN:

REASON FOR VISIT:

TREATMENT PLAN:

MEDICATIONS:

VACCINATIONS:

VISIT NOTES

Made in the USA
Middletown, DE
01 December 2024

65782841R10084